Old Baggy-Pants

Derek and Janey were eating jam
roly-poly in the hall and talking
about Mr Such's trousers. Mr Such
was their teacher and he wore the
same trousers to school, day in and
day out.

'They're so crumpled and baggy,'
Janey said.

'And grubby and thick,' said
Derek.

'Like a pair of old dish-cloths.'

'And he wears them all the time.'

'I don't think he's got any others.'

'Old Baggy-Pants, that's what he
is,' Derek added, sticking his fork into
his jam roly-poly.

'I wish he'd get some new ones,'
Janey sighed.

At that moment Old Baggy-Pants himself came into the hall. Janey's mouth fell open and Derek could see the mashed up jam roly-poly inside.

'What's up?' he said.

Janey blinked and pointed. There was Mr Such in a brand new suit. A spotless white suit without a crease in it. Everyone in the hall stopped eating and stared at him.

'Carry on, everyone,' said Mr Such, a bit red in the face. 'Carry on eating.'

'Wow!' said Derek, leaning across his plate. 'He looks so different.'

'He looks smart,' said Janey firmly. 'And about time, too.'

Later that afternoon Janey's class trooped back into the hall for P.E.

'I like the suit, sir,' Janey told Mr Such as they filed in.

'Thank you, Janey. It's for Parents' Evening, really.'

'Parents' Evening?'

'Yes, I have to look my best for that, don't I?'

'But that's not till Monday, Mr Such,' Derek said.

'I know that, Derek. I'm just getting used to it.'

While they were talking, Mrs Venn came out of the kitchen with a bowl of custard in her arms.

She was so shocked to see Mr Such in his bright new suit she gave a little jump. 'Oh my gosh!' she cried.

She grabbed one of the hall curtains to steady herself. The custard looped into the air, straight for Mr Such.

Derek saw it coming and stepped smartly in the way. The custard wobbled through the air and flopped against Derek's vest. Everyone fell silent. Derek stood there, looking sad and stunned. And covered in cold custard.

'Well done, Derek,' said Mr Such.
'You've saved my brand new suit.'

Derek tried to smile but by then the custard was oozing into his shorts.

After break, Mr Such changed back into his dish-cloth trousers.

'Please keep clear of this,' he said, hanging his new suit on the cupboard door. 'Keep well clear.'

A lovely green colour

The last lesson of the day was art. They
had to paint interesting faces. Janey
was doing a monster. She put blood-shot
bits in his eyes, a bolt through his neck
and green stuff coming out of his nose.
She was pleased with the green stuff,
but she'd mixed up too much. She
asked Derek if he wanted some.

'I don't need any green stuff, Janey,'
he said. 'I'm doing a footballer.'

'Well, he could have green stuff coming out of his nose, couldn't he?' she said.

'No,' said Derek. 'He couldn't.'

'You could use it for the background. Like grass.'

'I'm not having my footballer running around on green stuff from a monster's nose, thank you,' said Derek.

He nudged Janey's elbow, and green stuff spilled over the desk.

He tried to stop it trickling onto the floor.

Then he reached behind him and rubbed his hands on the towel. Except that it wasn't the towel.

'Oh,' he said quietly. 'What have I done?'

Janey could see what had happened. Derek had wiped his hands on Mr Such's new trousers.

'You've done it now,' she said. 'Old Baggy-Pants'll go up the wall when he sees this.'

Mr Such was on the other side of the room. He looked up and smiled at them.

'Are you getting on all right, you two?' he asked.

'Yes, thank you, sir,' said Janey brightly.

She didn't dare tell him the truth.

She grabbed some paper and started to rub at the green marks.

'You daft clod,' said Derek, 'you're making them worse. They're twice as big now.'

13

They were. Janey looked at Derek and thought hard.

'There's only one thing for it now,' she said.

'What's that?'

'Put them back on the hanger. Then we can clean them up after school.'

When Mr Such came over to look at their pictures, the suit was still swinging slightly on the cupboard door.

'Oh,' he said. 'I love that shade of green, Janey. That's a lovely colour.'

At home time Mr Such pottered around for ages and would not leave them on their own. They stacked chairs as slowly as chairs have ever been stacked. Then, at last, he wandered off to the staffroom.

Derek darted over to the sink and turned on the taps. Janey grabbed the trousers and flung them across the room at him. He caught them and plunged them into the sink. He grabbed a plastic bottle and squirted it hard at the trousers.

'What are you doing?' Janey yelled.

'Washing-up liquid,' said Derek.
'That'll get stains out.'

'That's not washing-up liquid, Derek.
That's glue.'

Almost at once they heard Mr Such
outside the door. He came in wearing
his anorak and cycle clips. Derek and
Janey stood side by side in front of the
sink.

'Oh,' said Mr Such. 'Are you still
here?'

'Nearly finished, sir,' Janey said, and tried to smile.

'Well, it looks tidy to me. I should run off home now.'

He went over to the jacket on the cupboard door.

'Don't,' said Derek.

'Don't what?'

'Don't take the suit.'

'Why ever not?'

'Because... because...'

17

'Because you might get it dirty,'
Janey said. 'It'll be safer if you leave it
here. Won't it, Derek?'

Derek nodded. Mr Such looked
puzzled. His hand was still half way to
the jacket.

'It might fall off your bike,' Janey
added. 'And land on a heap of rubbish
or something.'

Mr Such lowered his hand.

'Well,' he said, 'you might be right. I
don't want any more accidents.'

When he'd gone, they put the
trousers in a plastic bag and smuggled
them off to Derek's house.

They threw the trousers in the
kitchen sink and covered them with
hot water and washing powder. They
scrubbed them with a stiff brush, a bar
of soap and a wiry thing. The water
foamed into a pile of bubbles as high
as their elbows.

'Is it working?' Janey asked.

Derek flapped the bubbles
out of the way and looked into
the sink.

'Still green,' he groaned.

'They squirted washing-up liquid,
polish and floor cleaner in the sink, but
they didn't work either.

'Maybe we should bash them about
like a washing machine,' said Derek.

So they ran outside and bashed the trousers up and down on Derek's garden path. But that just picked up more dirt. And Janey thought they were beginning to shrink.

'There's only one thing for it now,' she said.

'What's that?'

'We'll have to take them to the dry-cleaners.'

The hero

Next day was Saturday. Derek and
Janey caught the first bus into town. The
trousers sat on the seat between them,
screwed up tight in a plastic bag. Janey
could hardly bear to look at them.

They waited till the dry-cleaners
was empty and then marched in.
Janey smiled at the girl and the girl
smiled back.

'The trousers, Derek,' Janey said.

'What about them?'

'Hand them over.'

'I can't.'

'Why not?'

'Because you've got them.'

'No I haven't. You have.'

For a moment or two they stood there staring at each other. Then Derek blinked and said in a quiet voice, 'Janey, they're still on the bus.'

Three hours later, tired and fed up, they arrived at the bus station. They walked up and down till they saw their bus. It was parked in a corner of the yard with two feet sticking out from under it.

'Excuse me,' Janey said to the feet, 'we left something on your bus this morning.'

The feet wriggled out and a man stood up, blinking. He wiped his hands on an oily rag.

'What was it?' he said.

24

'A pair of trousers,' said Derek.

'No,' said the man. 'I haven't seen any trousers on this bus. Only the ones people were wearing.'

He shook his head and tossed the oily rag into a box. As it sailed through the air, a leg unfolded from the grubby bundle. A leg with green stains on it.

'There they are!' Janey cried.

'Well, well, well,' said the man. 'I never noticed that before.'

25

Derek fished the trousers out of the box on the end of a spanner. He held them up to examine them.

'Oh dear,' he said. 'They're worse than ever.' Janey sighed.

'There's only one thing for it now,' she said.

'What's that?'

'We'll have to own up.'

On Monday Derek and Janey got to school early. They slipped into the classroom and took the trousers out of the bag.

They saw the oil from the bus and the dirt from Derek's garden. They saw the glue and the green paint. They looked at each other and sighed.

'We have to do it,' said Janey. 'We have to tell the truth.'

Then they put the trousers back on the hanger and went off to look for Mr Such.

They found him in the hall.

'Janey, Derek,' said Mr Such with a smile. 'What's all this?'

'It's your suit, Mr Such,' Janey said bravely. 'We've got something to tell you.'

But before she could say another word, Mrs Venn burst into the hall and grabbed Mr Such by his arm.

'Chips! Chips!' she screamed.

'No thank you, Mrs Venn,' said Mr Such. 'It's too early in the morning for chips.'

'No, no, Mr Such. The chips in the kitchen! They're on fire!'

'What?'

Mr Such hurried over to the kitchen doors and pushed them open. A cloud of blue smoke rolled into the hall.

'My word!' he said, and backed away again.

'Chuck some water on it, sir!' squeaked Derek.

'You can't do that,' said Mr Such. 'Water will make it worse. I need a cloth or something to smother the flames.'

Then he saw the suit dangling on its hanger from Janey's finger.

'I think there's only one thing for it, Mr Such,' said Janey, and Mr Such grabbed the suit.

Of course the suit was ruined. It turned into a mangled mess of smoke and grease. Janey tried to tell Mr Such about the green stains and how they tried to clean them off. But Mr Such didn't really listen.

'Never mind,' he kept saying. 'Never mind about that.'

Mr Such was the hero of the hour so he was rather pleased with himself. The head promised him another brand new suit and he was pleased with that, too.

'Jolly good,' said Mr Such. 'I can get a nice, bright white one.'

'Oh, don't do that,' said Janey quickly.

'Why ever not?'

'Well, we think green would suit you better, don't we, Derek?'

'Much better,' Derek nodded. 'We think green's a lovely colour.'

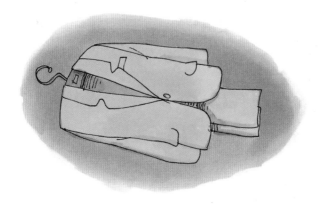

About the author

While I was teaching, I
enjoyed drama and reading
books aloud with children.
This encouraged me to write
and since then I have
written a number of scripts
for radio, stage and
television, around a baker's
dozen or so – that is, thirteen – children's
books. I can't ever remember wearing a
white suit at school. It would have been
asking for trouble.

I enjoy reading, almost anything to do with
cricket, and cycling around Cambridge,
where I live with my family.